THE LITTLE BOOK OF
FERMENTED FOODS

Other Books by Lynda Balslev

The Little Book of Fika

The Little Book of Whiskey

The Little Book of Cheese and Charcuterie

The Little Book of Dumplings

THE LITTLE BOOK OF FERMENTED FOODS

The Funky World Where Food Is Alive and Good Gut Health Thrives

LYNDA BALSLEV

Andrews McMeel
PUBLISHING®

CONTENTS

Fermentation
and civilization
are inseparable.

—JOHN CIARDI

INTRODUCTION

THE MAGIC OF FERMENTATION—AN ANCIENT PRACTICE FOR MODERN WELLNESS

For thousands of years, people across cultures have been fermenting foods—not only to preserve them but to unlock hidden flavors, boost nutrition, and improve digestion. From spicy kimchi and nutty cheeses to effervescent kombucha and umami-rich miso, fermented foods are more than just tasty; they are powerful tools for good health.

This book is a guide to fermentation. It will help to explain how the process of fermentation works, how it can enhance your diet, and how it can boost your overall health. It explains the origins of fermentation as a universal preservation method and culinary tradition, and it provides an atlas of fermented specialties from around the globe with approachable recipes, along with practical tips for DIY fermenting at home.

Welcome to the world of fermentation—where the food is alive and good health begins in the gut.

> What fermentation shows us is the invisible connections of everything.
>
> —**MERCEDES VILLALBA**

THE LIVING ART OF FERMENTATION

PAST, PURPOSE, AND PRACTICE

Fermentation never wants to be consistent. . . . The fact that we have different styles of fermented foods *is* that idea in the flesh . . . [it is] chaos theory lived out. . . . People are realizing this was always a power that was in our hands. . . . And that's the beauty of it.

—DAVID ZILBER

A BRIEF HISTORY

Fermentation is one of the oldest methods to preserve food. Long before refrigeration or canning existed, people relied on fermentation to transform fresh, perishable ingredients into flavorful, nutritious foods that could be stored for months through seasons of scarcity.

The ability to securely store food gave early societies the means to transition from nomadic hunting and gathering to settled farming communities. Fermented foods provided sustenance during migrations, ensured nutrition through the winter, and created portable provisions for travel and trade. Beyond practicality, the shared rituals of fermenting and storing food became cultural traditions, binding communities together and laying the groundwork for social growth.

> Fermentation may have been a better invention than fire.
>
> **—DAVID WALLACE**

Some of the earliest archaeological evidence of fermentation includes 13,000-year-old beer residue found in Israel; traces of fermented milk from animals, such as camels, goats, sheep, and cattle, dating back to around 10,000 BCE in the Middle East and Central Asia; and fermented rice, honey, and fruit discovered in Neolithic China from around 7000 BCE.

Fast-forward to the nineteenth century, when our understanding of fermentation changed dramatically, thanks to the French scientist Louis Pasteur. He proved that fermentation is driven by living microorganisms like yeast, which grow, multiply, and organize themselves during the process. This discovery helped to make fermentation more efficient and reliable by transforming what was a previously mysterious and unpredictable process into one that could be studied and optimized.

In the early twentieth century, the scientist Élie Metchnikoff linked fermented foods—especially those containing lactic acid bacteria, like yogurt—to health benefits such as digestion and longevity. This led to the concept of probiotics: live microorganisms that, when eaten in the right amounts, support our health.

As science advanced, we learned more about how these microbes not only preserve and flavor food but also improve gut health and boost immunity. By the late twentieth century, prebiotics were identified as certain types of undigestible dietary fiber that are food for gut microbes (probiotics), which provided the framework central to microbiome research. Today, many probiotic-rich fermented foods are specifically crafted to include beneficial bacteria for both flavor and health, such as yogurt, kefir, kimchi, and kombucha.

Since the most ancient times, all men, and particularly those endeavored in the practice of medicine, have brought closer together two natural phenomena of capital importance: illness or fever and fermentation.

—LOUIS PASTEUR

THE POWER OF FERMENTATION

Fermentation doesn't just preserve food—it transforms it into something more digestible, nutritious, and flavorful. It introduces probiotics, the beneficial microbes that support a healthy gut. These probiotics become part of the gut microbiome, the diverse community of microbes that live in the digestive system.

HEALTH BENEFITS

A healthy microbiome plays a crucial role in digestion and nutrient absorption, helps produce essential vitamins, strengthens the immune system, reduces inflammation, protects against harmful bacteria, and supports mental well-being. When we eat fermented foods, we feed our internal ecosystem and unlock a host of health benefits.

Here's how fermentation works for you:

1. Improves Digestibility

Microbes break down complex starches, proteins, and fibers into simpler forms our bodies can easily absorb.

Example: In sourdough bread, fermentation partially digests gluten, making it gentler on digestion.

2. Boosts Vitamin Content

Certain bacteria and yeasts produce vitamins during fermentation.

Example: Fermented foods are often higher in B vitamins and may provide vitamin K_2, which supports bone health.

3. Unlocks Minerals

Fermentation breaks down phytates—compounds that block minerals—making nutrients more available.

Example: Fermented soy, grains, and legumes offer more absorbable iron, zinc, and calcium than their raw forms.

4. Creates Beneficial Compounds

The fermentation process produces peptides, organic acids, and antioxidants that can support immunity and reduce inflammation.
Example: Fermented dairy releases peptides linked to healthier blood pressure.

5. Supports Gut Health

Fermented foods deliver live microbes that help keep the gut microbiome balanced and resilient.
Example: Yogurt, kefir, kimchi, sauerkraut, and kombucha deliver probiotics that nourish beneficial gut bacteria.

Naturally, fermented foods are your friends!

—ANDREW WEIL

MEET THE MICROBES

Fermentation involves three categories of microorganisms: bacteria, yeast, and mold.

Lactic acid fermentation is carried out by lactic acid bacteria, which convert sugars into lactic acid. This process imparts a tangy, acidic flavor, promotes the growth of probiotics, and helps preserve food. Common examples include kimchi, pickles, sauerkraut, yogurt, kefir, and fermented cereals.

Alcoholic fermentation is a process in which yeasts convert sugars into alcohol and carbon dioxide. This process not only produces alcohol but also creates natural carbonation.

It's fundamental to making foods and beverages such as bread, kvass, beer, cider, and wine.

Acetic acid fermentation is a process in which alcohol is converted into acetic acid by specific bacteria. This fermentation imparts a distinct tangy, acidic flavor and acts as a natural preservative. Common examples of this method include vinegar, pickles, kombucha, and cocoa.

Alkaline fermentation occurs when *Bacillus subtilis* breaks down proteins into amino acids, peptides, and ammonia. This process develops deep umami flavors and soft, sticky textures. An example is Japanese natto (fermented soybeans).

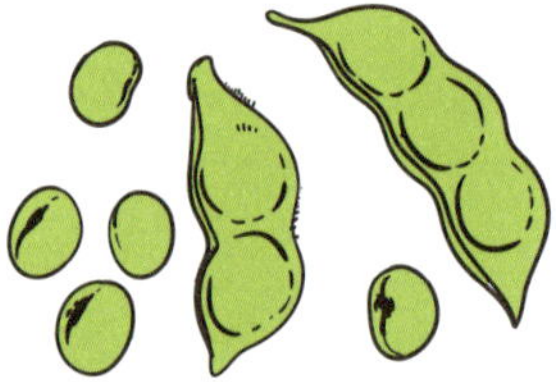

Mold is a type of fungus used in fermentation. Certain molds, such as *Aspergillus, Rhizopus,* and *Penicillium,* break down complex carbohydrates and proteins into simpler, flavorful compounds. Some also contribute to the fermentation of alcohol and acids, such as sake (Japanese rice wine). Molds play a crucial role in various food fermentations, such as miso, soy sauce, tempeh, and certain cheeses.

To ferment your own
food is to lodge a small
but eloquent protest—
on behalf of the senses
and the microbes—against
the homogenization
of flavors and food
experiences.

—MICHAEL POLLAN

"Culture" and "culture" mean two different things to a biologist and an anthropologist, but in fermentation, they overlap completely.

—DAVID ZILBER

FLAVOR MAGIC

The process of fermentation elevates the flavor and enhances the texture of food while coaxing out aromas that would otherwise remain hidden. Here are a few examples:

1. ENHANCES UMAMI

Umami is one of the five tastes, which also include sweet, sour, salty, and bitter. Fermentation deepens savory umami notes by breaking down proteins into amino acids such as glutamate, which creates deep flavor. Umami is what gives aged cheese its depth of flavor, soy sauce its intensity, and miso its savory qualities; it contributes savory notes to kimchi and fermented fish sauces as well.

2. MELLOWS SHARPNESS

Sour, sharp flavors soften and gain complexity through fermentation. Preserved lemons lose their puckery sharpness and develop floral notes. Sourdough bread and aged vinegars become more rounded and cohesive in flavor.

3. REDUCES BITTERNESS

Fermentation smooths out harsh bitterness. Cacao beans used for chocolate and green coffee beans are fermented to reduce bitterness and amplify nuanced flavors. Fermented brassicas, such as cabbage in sauerkraut, become sweeter and milder.

4. AMPLIFIES BRIGHTNESS

The tang of lactic acid fermentation adds brightness to foods such as yogurt, kefir, and buttermilk. It provides a vibrant zing and refreshing effervescence to kimchi, fermented pickles, and kombucha.

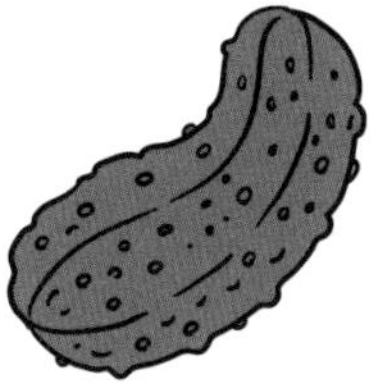

5. INTENSIFIES AROMA

Fermentation releases aromas, from the fruity, floral notes of fruits and vegetables to the nutty, earthy scent of tempeh, to the funky notes of cheese and cured meats. These scents are the result of microbial activity breaking down fats and proteins into fragrant compounds.

While conversion of sugars to ethanol is the predominant reaction, it is only one of potentially thousands of biochemical reactions taking place during fermentation. . . . Wine is, in fact, one of the most complex of all beverages: the fruit of a soil, climate, and vintage, digested by a fungus through a process guided by the culture, vision, and skill of an individual man or woman.

—NEEL BURTON

FERMENTING AT HOME

SIMPLE TIPS AND BASIC RULES

1. CLEANLINESS

- Ensure that all work surfaces, equipment, utensils, and your hands are thoroughly clean to prevent unwanted bacteria.
- Sanitize equipment by cleaning with hot, soapy water or running through the dishwasher.
- Wear gloves when handling the food.
- When tasting, always use a clean utensil.

2. INGREDIENTS

- Choose the freshest produce, organic when possible; wash it well in cold water and thoroughly dry.
- Avoid blemished or bruised produce, which may contain pathogens.
- Use only noniodized salt, such as kosher salt or sea salt. Avoid table salt with caking agents.
- Use filtered water when possible. Avoid chlorinated water, as the chlorine can kill beneficial bacteria.

3. EQUIPMENT

- Glass jars (mason or Kilner) are nonreactive and allow you to see the fermentation process. Use for small-batch ferments like pickles, kimchi, sauerkraut, garlic, and hot sauce.
- Ceramic crocks are ideal for large batches. Use for large-batch ferments of sauerkraut or whole pickles.
- Airlock lids are specialized lids used in fermentation, particularly with mason jars, that allow carbon dioxide (CO_2) to escape during the fermentation process while preventing oxygen and other contaminants from entering.

- Fermentation weights sit on top of your ferment and weigh down the ferment below the brine. Examples include a single stone, a glass disk, or glass pebbles.
- When using metal utensils for fermenting, use stainless steel, which is nonreactive and easy to sanitize. Stainless steel is generally the superior choice for fermentation utensils and lids because of its durability, hygiene, and nonreactive nature.

- When using plastic utensils, use utensils made from food-grade plastics. Note that with long-term fermenting, plastics can absorb and retain odors. Food-grade plastic lids can be a good, affordable option for shorter fermentations, particularly when paired with glass jars.
- Ensure that all containers and utensils are thoroughly cleaned and sanitized before and after each use to prevent contamination.
- Use an oven thermometer to check and monitor the oven temperature when relying on the oven light or pilot light for fermentation.

I truly believe in
fermentation
as a way to make
cooking easier.
It's a natural process
and way of being,
and ultimately the
future of cooking.

—RENÉ REDZEPI

GETTING STARTED

Keep it simple. Take your time. Embrace the process.

Make sure you have everything on hand and cleaned before you start.

Follow the recipe for precise measurements, method, and storage requirements.

Check the fermentation daily.

Refrigerate when ready to slow the fermentation process.

ACTIVE FERMENTATION

Don't store fermenting foods in direct sunlight or near a heat source. Too much heat can cause spoilage or mushy textures. Too much cold will slow or stall fermentation. The ideal temperature is between 68°F and 72°F (20°C and 22°C).

Use glass, ceramic, or food-grade plastic containers. Avoid reactive metals, such as aluminum.

Keep the ferment covered but allow gas to escape. Use a loose lid, a clean cloth with a rubber band, or a fermentation airlock lid (according to the manufacturer's instructions) to allow CO_2 to escape while keeping out dust and bugs.

Fully submerge the ferment in brine for wet ferments. Ensure that the ferment stays fully submerged under the brine to prevent mold growth. Use weights if needed.

Don't overfill jars—leave space. I usually leave about 1 inch of space at the top for gases to build and escape during fermentation.

STORAGE

Make sure the food is completely submerged in brine before storing.

Once the fermentation is to the desired flavor, tang, and texture, store in the refrigerator or a cool cellar (below 50°F/10°C). The cold slows fermentation but will not stop it completely.

Keep it airtight. Switch to airtight lids to prevent oxygen exposure (which can lead to mold growth) and to preserve texture and flavor.

Label jars with the start and storage dates to track aging.

Don't repeatedly open and expose finished ferments to air; it will shorten their shelf life.

> The trick to fermentation . . . is to manage a busy, chaotic world of microorganisms . . . in a way that creates something first, safe, and then utterly delicious.
>
> —LARRY NGUYEN

WHAT TO LOOK FOR AND WHAT TO AVOID

GOOD SIGNS

- Bubbles and effervescence are natural and a good sign of active fermentation.
- Ferments should smell pleasantly funky, not rotten. Pleasant aromas can range from tangy, sour, and yeasty to fruity, depending on what is fermenting.
- Gradual color and textural changes are normal. Vegetables may become duller or more translucent. Vegetables should soften slightly but retain some crunch. Liquids may thicken.
- A cloudy brine (for wet ferments) is typical and harmless.
- A flat white film (Kahm yeast) is harmless and can be skimmed off.

WHAT TO AVOID

- A rotten, foul, or decaying smell indicates contamination.
- Any fuzzy mold or colorful mold (black, pink, blue, green) on the surface is a sign of spoilage.
- Sliminess (beyond normal softness) suggests undesirable bacterial growth.
- Thick, viscous, stringy liquid is a sign of spoilage.
- No signs of fermentation activity when there should be (such as bubbling or an aroma) signifies that the fermentation is not working.

Bottom line: Trust your senses. If it looks, smells, or feels off, do not eat it. Discard it.

To ferment is to collaborate—with time, with nature, and with tradition.

—UNKNOWN

LET THE FERMENT BEGIN

Use these tips and tools to dive into fermenting at home. Immerse yourself in the spicy, sour, funky, fizzy world of fermentation with recipes from across the globe—each one a reflection of culture, ingenuity, and resilience. Created from simple ingredients and transformed by microbes and time, these foods share the universal language of fermentation.

It's actually an amazing feeling to wait for something to ferment. It runs totally contrary to the spirit of the modern day.

—RENÉ REDZEPI

GLOBAL FERMENTED RECIPES

RECIPES

ASIA

Traditional fermented ingredients:
rice, soybeans, cabbage, tea, chiles

KOREAN KIMCHI

Makes 1 quart

Fermentation time: 1 to 3 days

Kimchi is a traditional Korean condiment and side dish made by salting and fermenting vegetables—typically cabbage and radish. The process begins with a salty brine that inhibits harmful bacteria, allowing beneficial probiotics like *Lactobacillus* to thrive. These microbes convert natural sugars into lactic acid, giving kimchi its distinct sour-and-salty flavor. In addition to its probiotic benefits, kimchi is a rich source of fiber, vitamins, and antioxidants.

Serve kimchi as an accompaniment or side dish to rice, eggs, or noodles, or swirl it into soups and stews. Daikon radish and *gochugaru* (red chili powder) are available in Asian specialty stores and well-stocked supermarkets.

Special equipment

1 or 2 kitchen towels
Salad spinner (optional)
Food prep gloves
1-quart glass jar with lid or airlock lid

Ingredients

1 large head napa cabbage (2 to 2½ pounds)
2 tablespoons kosher salt
5 garlic cloves, grated
¼ cup gochugaru (Korean red chili powder)
2 tablespoons fish sauce
1 tablespoon peeled and grated fresh ginger
1 tablespoon sugar
1 (4-inch) daikon radish, peeled, cut into matchsticks
4 scallions, sliced into 1-inch pieces

1. Quarter the cabbage lengthwise. Cut each length crosswise into 1½-inch pieces. Place the cabbage in a large bowl. Sprinkle the salt and toss well to combine. Cover the bowl with a kitchen towel and let stand at room temperature for 2 hours, stirring once or twice.

2. Combine the garlic, *gochugaru,* fish sauce, ginger, and sugar in a small bowl and whisk to blend.

(continued)

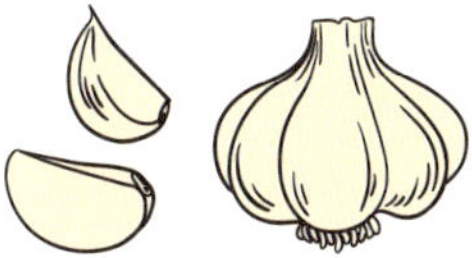

3. Drain the cabbage and rinse under cold water to remove the salt. Blot dry with a clean kitchen towel or spin dry in a salad spinner. Transfer the cabbage to a clean bowl and add the daikon, scallions, and the *gochugaru* sauce. With gloved hands, massage the sauce into the cabbage.

4. Pack the kimchi into the jar, pressing down on the cabbage until the liquid (brine) covers the cabbage, leaving about 1 inch of space at the top. Loosely seal the jar or use an airlock lid following the manufacturer's instructions and let the kimchi stand at room temperature (65°F to 75°F/18°C to 24°C) for 1 to 3 days. Check the kimchi once a day and taste for your desired level of tang and pungency. Use a clean spoon to resubmerge any vegetables in the liquid. When to your desired taste, seal the jar tightly and store in the refrigerator for up to 2 months.

KOREAN GOCHUJANG-MARINATED CHICKEN THIGHS

Serves 4

Gochujang is a traditional Korean fermented red chili paste made from *gochugaru*, glutinous rice and malt, fermented soybeans (*meju*), and salt. Its complex fermentation process involves lactic acid bacteria, which break down carbohydrates to create a subtle sourness, while enzymes from the soybeans and barley contribute sweetness and rich umami depth.

Sweet, spicy, and savory, gochujang adds bold flavor to sauces, marinades, soups, and stews. Use it to glaze or marinate meats like chicken, beef, or pork, or brush it on tofu and vegetables for roasting or grilling. Gochujang is widely available in Asian markets and well-stocked supermarkets, and it keeps well in the refrigerator for up to a year.

Gochujang is the star of this fiery marinade, imparting a unique blend of sweetness, spiciness, and umami flavor to the chicken while coating it with a brick-red glaze.

(continued)

Marinade

¼ cup gochujang paste
2 tablespoons soy sauce
2 tablespoons unseasoned rice vinegar
2 tablespoons packed dark brown sugar
1 tablespoon filtered water
1 tablespoon toasted sesame oil
1 teaspoon peeled and finely grated fresh ginger
1 garlic clove, finely grated

Chicken Thighs

8 bone-in, skin-on chicken thighs
Chopped scallions, for garnish
Toasted sesame seeds, for garnish
Cooked rice, for serving

1. Whisk the marinade ingredients in a small bowl until smooth. Set aside ¼ cup for basting.

2. Place the chicken thighs in a large resealable plastic bag. Pour in the marinade and massage the bag to thoroughly coat the chicken. Seal the bag and refrigerate for at least 1 hour or up to 24 hours.

3. Heat the oven to 375°F and line a baking sheet with parchment paper or foil. Remove the chicken from the bag, letting any excess marinade drip back into the bag. Discard the bag.

4. Arrange the chicken on the baking sheet. Roast until a meat thermometer inserted in the thickest part without touching the bone registers 165°F.

5. While the chicken is cooking, gently warm the reserved marinade in a small saucepan over medium-low heat. Brush the chicken with some of the glaze during the last few minutes of cooking.

6. Garnish with scallions and sesame seeds, and serve with rice.

JAPANESE MISO

Makes about 4 cups miso paste

Fermentation time: 1 to 3 months

Miso is a fermented soybean paste and a staple of Japanese cuisine. It's made by fermenting soybeans with salt and koji, a type of mold that breaks down starches and proteins to develop miso's signature flavor. The result is a deeply savory paste with sweet, salty, rich umami notes. Miso is used in everything from soups to marinades, dressings, and sauces.

Miso comes in a range of colors that reflect its ingredients and fermentation time. The longer the fermentation, the darker and more intense the flavor. White miso is mildest and sweetest, yellow miso offers a balance of sweet and savory, and red miso is saltiest and has the boldest, most complex umami flavor.

Koji rice (malted rice) is available online or in Asian specialty markets or well-stocked supermarkets.

Special equipment

Potato masher or food processor
Food prep gloves
1-quart glass jar with lid or airlock lid
Fermentation weights

Ingredients

2 cups dried soybeans
2 cups koji rice
½ cup plus ½ teaspoon kosher salt, divided

1. Rinse the soybeans and drain, then transfer to a large bowl and cover with 4 inches of filtered water. Soak the soybeans for 12 to 18 hours at room temperature.

2. Drain the soybeans, then transfer to a large pot and cover with 2 inches of filtered water. Bring to a boil, then decrease the heat and simmer uncovered for 2 to 3 hours, until the soybeans are very soft, adding more water as needed to keep the soybeans submerged.

(continued)

3. Combine the koji rice and ½ cup of the salt in a large bowl. Mix with clean hands to combine.

4. Drain the soybeans, reserving 1 cup cooking water; cool the water to room temperature.

5. Place the soybeans in a large clean bowl and mash them with a potato masher (or place them in a food processor and process, in batches, to form a thick paste). If the paste is too dry, add a little of the reserved cooking water to moisten. Let the mashed soybeans cool to lukewarm or room temperature (if they are hot, they will kill the koji).

6. Add the soybeans to the koji mixture. Mix with clean hands to combine. Add only a small amount of the reserved cooking water to slightly moisten if needed.

7. Using gloves and working with a handful at a time, roll the mixture into balls. Pack the balls into the jar, one at a time, mashing each ball down to remove any air pockets. Press

tightly after each addition and repeat with the remaining 1½-inch balls. Leave about 1 inch of space at the top. Sprinkle the top with the remaining ½ teaspoon salt. Completely cover with plastic wrap, then place fermentation weights on top of the plastic wrap to weigh down the miso.

8. Loosely seal the jar or use an airlock lid following the manufacturer's instructions. Place it in a cool, dark location, such as a basement or the back of a closet, for 1 month. After about 4 weeks the miso should be salty, sweet, and mild. After about 3 months it will be darker and stronger. When ready, seal the jar tightly and store in the refrigerator for up to 1 year.

A dark liquid will form on top of the miso while it ferments. This is tamari (a gluten-free soy sauce). Any amount that is collected can be used as a condiment or flavoring ingredient in the same way as you would use soy sauce.

MISO SPINACH SOUP

Serves 3 to 4

Using dashi packets is an easy shortcut to making homemade miso soup. Add the packets to hot water and let them steep, as you would a teabag. Dashi packets can be purchased online or in Asian specialty markets.

Ingredients

3½ cups filtered water
2 (10-g) dashi packets
¼ cup white or yellow miso paste
3 to 4 ounces shiitake mushrooms, ends trimmed, caps thinly sliced
3 ounces fresh baby spinach leaves, torn if large
6 ounces soft tofu, cut into ½-inch cubes
2 scallions, white and green parts thinly sliced

1. Combine the water and dashi packets in a large saucepan to make a broth. Bring to a simmer over medium heat. Cover and reduce the heat to medium-low and let simmer for 3 to 4 minutes. Carefully discard the packets without turning off the heat.

2. Transfer ½ cup warm dashi broth to a small bowl. Add the miso and whisk to blend.

3. Add the mushrooms to the saucepan and simmer for 3 to 4 minutes. Add the spinach and stir for 15 to 30 seconds, until wilted. Remove from the heat.

4. Whisk the miso-broth mixture into the soup, then gently stir in the tofu and scallions. Return the pan to the heat and warm the soup over medium-low heat without letting it boil (which will destroy some of the nutrients in the miso).

5. Ladle into bowls and serve immediately.

JAPANESE NATTO RICE BOWL

Serves 2

Natto is a traditional Japanese food made from soybeans fermented with *Bacillus subtilis* bacteria. It has a distinctively pungent—some may say off-putting—smell, with a stringy, sticky texture. Natto has a savory, cheesy, nutty flavor and is rich in protein, vitamins, and minerals. Natto is often served as a breakfast food with warm rice. It can be purchased in Asian markets and Japanese supermarkets. If purchased frozen, let the natto defrost in the refrigerator overnight before using.

Ingredients

1 cup cooked sushi rice, warm
4 ounces prepared natto
1 avocado, diced
1 to 2 scallions, white and green parts, sliced
Soy sauce or tamari, for drizzling
Japanese hot mustard (karashi), for serving

Divide the rice between two serving bowls. Spoon half of the natto over each bowl of rice. Top with the remaining ingredients. Other toppings can include grated daikon, kimchi, diced cucumber, shredded dried nori seaweed, and sesame seeds.

CHINESE KOMBUCHA

Makes 1 gallon

Fermentation time: 1 to 2 weeks

Kombucha is a fermented black tea beverage that can be traced back to China to around 220 BC. Its fermentation process begins by combining sweetened black or green tea with a starter tea (previously fermented kombucha) and a SCOBY (a symbiotic culture of bacteria and yeast). The SCOBY feeds on the sugar in the sweetened tea and the acids present in the starter tea. As the culture gets to work, acetic, lactic, and alcoholic fermentation occur together, gradually transforming the tea into a tangy, slightly effervescent drink that is rich in probiotics as well as antioxidants from its tea base. SCOBYs are readily available online or at specialty retailers.

Special equipment

1-gallon glass jar
Cotton cloth and rubber band
Glass bottles with plastic caps

Ingredients

4 cups filtered water, plus 8 cups cool or cold filtered water, divided
4 bags black or green tea (not decaf)
1 cup organic cane sugar
1 SCOBY
2 cups kombucha starter tea (either from a previous batch or unpasteurized, unflavored store-bought kombucha)

1. Bring 4 cups of the water to a boil in a large pot. Turn off the heat and add the tea bags. Let steep for 15 minutes.

2. Add the sugar to the pot and stir to dissolve. Remove the tea bags.

3. Add the prepared tea to the jar. Add the remaining 8 cups cool or cold water to the tea. Let the liquid cool to room temperature.

(continued)

4. Add the SCOBY and the kombucha starter tea to the jar. Cover with the cloth and secure with the rubber band. Place the jar in a warm place (70°F to 85°F/21°C to 29°C) without direct sunlight and let it ferment for 1 week. Taste the kombucha and continue to let it ferment until it reaches your desired taste. It will become sharper with time.

5. When the kombucha is ready, remove the SCOBY and reserve 2 cups of the liquid to use as starter tea for your next batch. (Store the SCOBY in the reserved kombucha [starter tea] in a jar. Cover with the cloth and secure with the rubber band. Store in a dark place at room temperature [65°F to 75°F/18°C to 24°C]. Feed it by adding more sweet tea every 4 to 6 weeks. Check regularly for signs of mold on the SCOBY. Discard the SCOBY and the liquid if there is mold.) To flavor kombucha, see the note on page 52.

6. Transfer the fermented kombucha into glass bottles with plastic (not metal) caps. Leave 1 inch of space at the top of each bottle. Seal the bottles and let the kombucha ferment in a dark place at room temperature (65°F to 75°F/18°C to 24°C) for 2 to 4 more days. Check carbonation levels by twisting the caps. Once the kombucha is carbonated to your liking, move the bottles to the refrigerator to slow the fermentation and carbonation processes. The kombucha can be stored in the refrigerator for up to 2 months. Release the gas from the bottles (burp them) once a month.

(continued)

Note: To flavor kombucha, add puréed or chopped fresh or frozen fruit or fresh herbs during the second fermentation, after the SCOBY has been removed. Note that the sugar in the fruit will boost fermentation. Recommended ratios of fruit to kombucha are 10–30 percent fruit to 90–70 percent kombucha. The exact amounts are up to your taste and desired level of carbonation. Start with less and add more in future batches.

A healthy SCOBY (symbiotic culture of bacteria and yeast) is usually white or light brown and has a sweet-sour, vinegary smell. A bad SCOBY is typically identified by fuzzy, colored mold or a foul odor. If you see fuzzy, green, or black growth on the SCOBY, or if it has a putrid odor, it's likely moldy and should be discarded.

INDONESIAN TEMPEH

Makes 2 (14-ounce) cakes

Fermentation time: 24 to 48 hours

Tempeh is a staple of Indonesian cuisine. It's a fermented soybean product, typically formed into a dense cake or block. The soybeans are inoculated with a starter culture containing *Rhizopus* mold spores, then fermented at a warm temperature. As the mycelium grows, it binds the beans together into a dense white cake.

Tempeh has an earthy, nutty flavor and a firm texture. It's a rich vegetarian source of protein, fiber, vitamins, and minerals and contains probiotics that support gut health. Tempeh can be grilled, fried, baked, or steamed and works well in salads, stews, stir-fries, and sandwiches.

Special equipment

Metal skewer

2 (1-quart) resealable plastic bags

(continued)

Ingredients

16 ounces dried soybeans

2 tablespoons apple cider or white vinegar

1 teaspoon tempeh starter (*Rhizopus oligosporus* spores)

1. Place the soybeans in a large bowl and cover with 3 inches of filtered water. Let stand for 8 to 12 hours.

2. Rub the soybeans with your hands to remove most of the hulls (they will float). Discard the hulls. Drain and rinse the soybeans.

3. Transfer the soybeans to a large pot and cover with 2 inches of filtered water. Partially cover the pot and cook over medium heat for 30 to 45 minutes, until the soybeans are tender but not mushy. Drain the soybeans and spread them on a clean kitchen towel. Blot dry and cool completely.

4. Transfer the cooled soybeans to a bowl. Add the vinegar and stir to combine. Sprinkle the tempeh starter over the soybeans and stir to thoroughly combine.

5. Use the skewer to perforate the plastic bags with holes in 1-inch intervals. Divide the soybeans between the bags. Flatten the bags to about 1-inch thickness. Place the bags between two cutting boards and set them in a warm spot (80°F to 90°F/26°C to 32°C), such as an oven with the pilot light on, with the door cracked for air circulation.

6. Let ferment for 24 to 48 hours. The tempeh is ready when the entire surface is covered in white mold (mycelium) as well as in between the soybeans. It will resemble a cake. Remove it from the warm spot and cool to room temperature. (Note that black spots on the tempeh are okay. However, a slimy texture, a strong ammonia smell, or pink/green molds are signs of contamination, and the tempeh should be discarded.)

7. Store in the refrigerator in an airtight container for up to 1 week. To freeze, steam the tempeh for 20 minutes to stop the fermentation, then cool. Freeze in an airtight container for up to 3 months.

MARINATED AND ROASTED TEMPEH

Serves 4

Steaming tempeh before marinating and cooking helps to remove any natural bitterness and allows it to absorb more of the marinade. Once marinated and roasted, the tempeh can be served warm or cold.

Marinade

¼ cup soy sauce or tamari
2 tablespoons maple syrup or packed dark brown sugar
2 tablespoons rice vinegar
2 tablespoons toasted sesame oil
1 teaspoon sriracha

Tempeh

2 (8-ounce) blocks tempeh, cut into 1-inch cubes or wedges

1. Whisk the marinade ingredients in a small bowl.

2. In a large pot fitted with a steamer basket, bring 1 inch of water to a boil. Place the tempeh in the steamer for 10 to 12 minutes.

3. Arrange the steamed tempeh in one layer in a nonreactive baking dish. Pour the marinade over and turn the tempeh to coat. Refrigerate for at least 1 hour or up to 24 hours, turning the tempeh once or twice.

4. Heat the oven to 425°F and line a baking sheet with parchment paper.

5. Arrange the tempeh on the baking sheet and brush with some of the marinade. Bake for 20 to 25 minutes, until it turns a deep golden brown and begins to caramelize in spots, flipping once and basting once or twice with the marinade.

6. Serve the tempeh as is or add to salads, sandwiches, and wraps or rice and noodle dishes.

VIETNAMESE NEM CHUA FRIED RICE

Serves 4

Nem chua is a Vietnamese fermented pork dish. It's a popular appetizer, snack, and side dish especially enjoyed during Lunar New Year as a symbol of prosperity and togetherness.

Nem chua consists of ground pork cured with garlic, chiles, and spices, then wrapped in plastic or banana leaves and fermented, resulting in a salty, tangy flavor and a chewy texture.

It's typically consumed raw but remains safe to eat because of its lactic fermentation process. The process and inclusion of natural bacteria help to inhibit the growth of harmful pathogens. Prepared *nem chua* is available in Asian markets.

Ingredients

2 tablespoons vegetable oil, divided
6 ounces prepared nem chua, diced
6 scallions, white and green parts chopped, divided
1 medium carrot, peeled and finely diced
1 cup frozen peas, defrosted
2 garlic cloves, minced
2 large eggs, lightly whisked
1 tablespoon unsalted butter
4 cups cooked and cooled jasmine or basmati rice, preferably day-old
1 tablespoon soy sauce
1 tablespoon oyster sauce
2 teaspoons toasted sesame oil
1½ teaspoons fish sauce
½ teaspoon ground white pepper

1. Heat 1 tablespoon of the oil in a wok or large cast-iron skillet. Add the *nem chua* and cook for about 4 minutes, or until slightly brown. Transfer to a plate.

(continued)

2. If the pan is dry, add the remaining 1 tablespoon oil to the skillet. Add the scallion whites and carrot and sauté for about 2 minutes, or until the carrot is bright and crisp-tender. Stir in the peas and garlic and sauté for about 1 minute, or until the peas are bright and the garlic is fragrant. Push the vegetables to the side in the skillet and then add the eggs. Scramble for about 30 seconds, or until the eggs are just cooked through. Add the butter, rice, soy sauce, oyster sauce, sesame oil, fish sauce, and pepper and stir-fry until well combined.

3. Spread the mixture evenly in the pan and let it cook for 3 to 4 minutes, without stirring, to color and crisp on the bottom. Stir and repeat once or twice to achieve an even crispy texture. Serve garnished with the scallion greens.

FILIPINO ATCHARA

Makes 1 quart

Fermentation time: 1 day

Atchara is a Filipino condiment and side dish primarily made from green (unripened) papaya that is salted and soaked in a vinegar-based brine. The salt draws out moisture from the papaya, which then allows lactic acid bacteria to thrive. These beneficial bacteria convert sugars into lactic acid, resulting in a sweet and tangy flavor. Green papaya is rich in fiber, vitamin C, and antioxidants, which can aid digestion and boost the immune system. *Atchara* is served as a refreshing accompaniment to grilled meats and fried dishes or as part of Filipino breakfasts.

Special equipment

Kitchen towel or cheesecloth
1-quart glass jar with lid

(continued)

Ingredients

1 large green papaya, peeled and seeded, shredded (about 4 cups)

2 tablespoons plus 1 teaspoon kosher salt, divided

2 carrots, peeled and julienned

1 red bell pepper, seeded and julienned

1 jalapeño pepper, thinly sliced (and seeded, optional)

½ cup golden raisins

4 garlic cloves, thinly sliced

1 (2-inch) piece peeled fresh ginger, thinly sliced

2 cups unseasoned rice vinegar or white vinegar

1 cup granulated sugar

1. Combine the papaya and 2 tablespoons of the salt in a large bowl and toss to coat. Let stand at room temperature for 1 hour (or cover and refrigerate for up to 4 hours).

2. Drain the papaya. Wrap it in a kitchen towel and squeeze out as much liquid as possible. Place the papaya, carrots, peppers, raisins, garlic, and ginger in a large clean bowl and stir to combine. Transfer to the jar, leaving 1 inch of space at the top.

3. Combine the vinegar, sugar, and the remaining 1 teaspoon salt in a medium saucepan. Bring to a boil over medium-high heat, stirring to dissolve the sugar. Lower the heat and simmer for 5 minutes.

4. Pour the hot vinegar syrup over the vegetables so they are completely covered and submerged. Immediately seal the jar with an airtight lid. Cool to room temperature, then refrigerate for at least 1 day before serving. The *atchara* can be stored in the refrigerator for up to 2 months.

RECIPES

EUROPE AND RUSSIA

Traditional fermented ingredients:
cabbage, dairy, rye, fruit

SAUERKRAUT

Makes about 2 quarts

Fermentation time: 3 to 10 days

Sauerkraut is a fermented food made from finely shredded cabbage, typically preserved with salt. It's known for its sour flavor and is a popular side dish or condiment in German and Eastern European cuisine. Natural bacteria converts the cabbage's sugars into lactic acid during the fermentation process, which creates sauerkraut's characteristically tangy flavor.

Sauerkraut is rich in probiotics, which support gut health and digestion. It also provides essential vitamins and minerals, including vitamin C, vitamin K, and potassium.

Special equipment

Food prep gloves
2-quart glass jar with lid
Fermentation weight
Cotton cloth and rubber band or airlock lid

Ingredients

1 medium head green cabbage (about 3 pounds)
1½ tablespoons kosher salt
1 tablespoon caraway seeds (optional)

1. Remove and discard any wilted outer leaves of the cabbage. Remove two or three large fresh outer leaves and set them aside. Quarter the cabbage lengthwise and remove the core. Thinly slice the cabbage.

2. Combine the cabbage and salt in a large bowl and mix to combine. Cover the bowl and let the cabbage stand at room temperature for 15 minutes.

(continued)

3. With gloved hands, massage and squeeze the cabbage for 8 to 10 minutes, until it's watery and limp. If using the caraway seeds, mix them in.

4. Grab handfuls of the shredded cabbage and pack into the jar, pressing down to compress while allowing the liquid to pool over the cabbage. Keep packing tightly until the cabbage is about 2 inches from the top of the jar. Pour any remaining liquid released by the cabbage in the bowl into the jar to cover by about 1 inch, leaving 1 inch of space at the top.

5. Place one or two of the reserved cabbage leaves over the surface of the sauerkraut. Tuck the edges of the cabbage leaves down into the jar to help keep the cabbage submerged in the liquid. Add the fermentation weight on top of the cabbage leaves.

6. Cover the jar with the cloth and secure with the rubber band or use an airlock lid following the manufacturer's instructions. Place in a dark area at room temperature (65°F to 75°F/18°C to 24°C) and let it ferment for 3 to 10

days, checking daily and pressing on the weight to make sure the cabbage is submerged in the liquid to prevent mold from growing.

7. When the cabbage has fermented to your taste, remove the weight and fasten the lid. Store in the refrigerator for up to 2 months. Serve warm or cold, as a condiment or an accompaniment to sandwiches, roasted meat, and sausages, or simply on its own.

KVASS

Makes 5 quarts

Fermentation time: 14 to 24 hours

Kvass is a popular fermented beverage in Slavic and Baltic countries. It's typically made from rye bread that is darkly toasted, which gives the drink its characteristic dark color and malty flavor. The bread is fermented with the help of yeast, while sugar is added to feed the yeast and initiate fermentation. This natural fermentation process develops probiotics, which are beneficial bacteria that can support gut health and aid digestion.

Kvass is generally considered a nonalcoholic drink, although fermentation does produce a small amount of alcohol (usually between 0.5% and 1.0% ABV). Its flavor is sweet, tangy, and slightly fruity, with subtle earthy, malty notes.

Special equipment

Funnel

Plastic soda bottles

Ingredients

5 quarts (1¼ gallons) filtered water

8 ounces whole-grain rye bread, sliced, darkly toasted

½ cup raisins

1 cup granulated sugar

¾ tablespoon active dry yeast

1. Bring the water to a boil in a large heavy-bottom pot over high heat. Remove from the heat and add the bread and raisins. Cover the pot and let stand at room temperature for 8 to 12 hours.

2. Strain the bread and raisins from the pot. Combine the sugar and yeast in a small bowl, then stir into the pot. Cover the pot and let stand at room temperature (65°F to 75°F/18°C to 24°C) for 6 to 12 hours, stirring occasionally.

(continued)

3. Strain out any remaining solids from the liquid. Using a funnel, transfer to the plastic bottles and refrigerate until cold. Once cold, the kvass is ready to drink. The carbonation will develop to your taste the longer it ferments. Store in the refrigerator for up to 1 week. The kvass will continue to ferment and build up pressure, so use plastic bottles designed to hold pressurized beverages. After 2 days, burp the bottles once a day to avoid overcarbonation. The kvass will become more alcoholic the longer it ferments. Serve chilled with or without ice.

YOGURT

Makes 1 quart

Fermentation time: 6 to 12 hours

Yogurt is a dairy product made by fermenting milk with the addition of specific bacterial cultures, typically *Lactobacillus bulgaricus* and *Streptococcus thermophilus*. During fermentation, the bacteria convert the milk's natural sugars into lactic acid, which thickens the milk and gives yogurt its characteristic tangy flavor and creamy texture.

Homemade yogurt contains probiotics that support a healthy gut, reduce inflammation, and boost the immune system. It also provides essential nutrients such as calcium, protein, vitamins B_2 and B_{12}, and zinc. The fermentation process can also enhance the nutritional quality of the milk by increasing its protein content and boosting levels of vitamins B and C.

(continued)

Special equipment

Airtight storage container with lid

Ingredients

4 cups (1 quart) whole or 2% milk
2 tablespoons plain whole milk yogurt

1. Add the milk to a large heavy-bottom pot. Gently heat over medium heat until it reaches 180°F (82°C), stirring occasionally to prevent scorching.

2. Remove from the heat and cool to 110°F to 115°F (43°C to 46°C), stirring occasionally to prevent a skin from forming.

3. Transfer ¼ cup of the milk to a small bowl. Whisk the yogurt into the milk to blend. Return the yogurt mixture to the pot, whisking gently to combine. Cover the pot and transfer to a warm place (110°F to 115°F/38°C to 46°C), such as an oven with the pilot light on.

4. Let the yogurt stand until thick, 6 to 12 hours. The longer the yogurt stands, the thicker and tangier it will become.

5. When it reaches your desired taste and consistency, transfer the yogurt to an airtight storage container. Refrigerate the yogurt until it's chilled. Store for up to 2 weeks.

Note: To flavor the yogurt with fruit or honey, add when the yogurt has fermented and cooled.

KEFIR

Makes 4 cups

Fermenting time: 12 to 24 hours

Kefir is a traditional fermented milk drink that originated in the Caucasus Mountains of Eastern Europe. It's made by adding kefir grains—a symbiotic culture of beneficial bacteria and yeast—to milk. These cultures ferment the milk, producing a tangy, slightly effervescent drink with a thinner consistency than yogurt. Kefir grains can be purchased online or in health food stores.

Kefir is valued for its rich probiotic content, which supports gut health and digestion. It is also a good source of protein, calcium, and B vitamins. While cow's milk is commonly used, kefir can also be made from goat's milk or plant-based alternatives.

Special equipment

2 (1-quart) glass jars, one with lid
Cotton cloth and rubber band
Non-metal strainer

Ingredients

2 tablespoons active kefir grains
4 cups whole milk

1. Place the kefir grains in a jar. Add the milk, leaving about 1 inch of space at the top. Cover with the cloth and secure with the rubber band.

2. Let stand at room temperature (65°F to 75°F/18°C to 24°C) for 12 to 24 hours to ferment. It will have turned to kefir when the milk has thickened.

3. Using a non-metal strainer, strain the kefir into a separate clean jar and seal tightly. (The strained grains can be reused to make more kefir; transfer the grains to a cup of fresh milk and refrigerate until next use.) Store the kefir in the refrigerator for up to 1 week. Drink kefir on its own; use as a substitute for milk, yogurt, or buttermilk; or mix into cereals and smoothies.

CRÈME FRAÎCHE

Makes 2 cups

Fermentation time: 12 to 24 hours

Crème fraîche is a cultured cream that originated in France. It's made by adding a bacterial culture to heavy cream, allowing it to ferment and thicken naturally. The result is a rich, tangy, velvety cream with a smooth and luxurious texture. Because of its high fat content, crème fraîche is creamier and less tangy than sour cream and won't curdle when heated. Crème fraîche contains probiotics that support gut health, along with calcium and protein.

Special equipment

1 glass jar, large enough to hold the buttermilk and cream
Cotton cloth and rubber band

Ingredients

3 tablespoons cultured buttermilk or yogurt
2 cups (16 ounces) heavy cream

1. Combine the buttermilk and heavy cream in the jar. Cover with the cloth and secure with the rubber band. Let stand at room temperature (65°F to 75°F/18°C to 24°C) until thickened to your desired texture, 12 to 24 hours.

2. Transfer to the refrigerator and chill until cold. It will continue to thicken as it cools. Store the crème fraîche in the refrigerator for up to 1 week. Use it to thicken sauces; swirl it into pasta dishes, soups, mashes, and purées; and dollop it on fruit and desserts.

SPAGHETTI WITH LEMONY CRÈME FRAÎCHE SAUCE

Serves 4

A rich crème fraîche sauce adds creaminess and mild tang to this elegant pasta dish, which is brightened with lemon and fresh herbs. The spaghetti can be substituted with another pasta of your choice.

Ingredients

12 ounces spaghetti
2 tablespoons unsalted butter
1 garlic clove, grated
½ cup crème fraîche
1 teaspoon finely grated fresh lemon zest
2 to 3 tablespoons finely chopped fresh herbs, such as dill, chives, and/or chervil, plus more for garnish
¼ teaspoon freshly ground black pepper

1. Bring a large pot of salted water to a rolling boil. Add the pasta and cook until al dente according to package instructions. Scoop out ½ cup of the cooking water and set aside, then drain the pasta.

2. Melt the butter in a large skillet over medium heat. Add the garlic and stir for about 30 seconds, or until fragrant.

3. Add the drained pasta to the skillet with the reserved pasta water and the crème fraîche, stirring to thoroughly coat the pasta and emulsify the sauce. Stir in the lemon zest, fresh herbs, and pepper.

4. Serve immediately, garnished with additional fresh herbs.

So what does cheese evoke? Damp dark cellars, molds, mildews and mushrooms galore, dirty laundry and high school locker rooms. . . . In sum, cheese reminds of dubious, even unsavory places, both in nature and our own organisms. And yet we love it.

—MICHAEL POLLAN

SOURDOUGH BREAD

Makes 1 (9-inch) loaf

Sourdough is one of the oldest forms of leavened bread, with its origin tracing back to ancient Egypt. Before the use of commercial yeast, people relied on the wild yeasts and lactic acid bacteria naturally present in flour and the environment to make their bread rise. As the wild yeast and bacteria work together, they break down complex starches and gluten, making the bread easier to digest. The fermentation process also reduces phytic acid, which unlocks minerals such as iron and magnesium that are harder to absorb in other breads. The result is a loaf with a lower glycemic impact; a rich, tangy flavor; and a satisfying texture.

This recipe combines both yeast and sourdough starter to ensure a strong rise and the mildly tangy, soft loaf associated with sourdough bread. For best results, weigh the ingredients with a digital scale for precision. Sourdough starters can be purchased online or directly from bakeries.

(continued)

Ingredients

2½ cups (300 g) unbleached all-purpose flour or bread flour, plus more for dusting

¾ cup (170 g) filtered water, lukewarm

½ cup (113 g) active sourdough starter

1¼ teaspoons kosher salt

1 teaspoon instant yeast

Olive oil, for greasing

1. Combine all the ingredients except the olive oil in a large bowl or a stand mixer fitted with a dough hook. Mix and knead for 8 to 12 minutes by hand, or 5 to 10 minutes with a stand mixer, to make a soft, smooth dough.

2. Lightly oil a large clean bowl. Place the dough in the bowl and cover with plastic wrap. Let it rise at room temperature (65°F to 75°F/18°C to 24°C) for about 1 hour, or until doubled in size.

3. Transfer the dough to a lightly floured work surface. Gently deflate the dough and form into a ball by pulling the edges toward the center and turning it over, seam side down. Cover with a towel and let rest for 15 minutes.

4. Line a baking sheet with parchment paper and lightly oil a length of plastic wrap. Stretch the dough ball by rolling it back and forth to shape into a 9-inch oval. Transfer the dough to the baking sheet and cover lightly with the plastic wrap. Let the dough rise at room temperature (65°F to 75°F/18°C to 24°C) for about 1 hour, or until puffed.

(continued)

5. Heat the oven to 425°F/220°C. Lightly spray the loaf with water and dust with flour. Score the loaf by making two or three diagonal slashes across the top with a knife or lame (a double-sided blade for scoring bread). Bake the bread for about 30 minutes, or until golden brown.

6. Remove the bread from the oven and transfer it to a rack to cool. The bread can be stored at room temperature, loosely wrapped, for up to 2 days or frozen for up to 3 months.

God made yeast, as well as dough, and loves fermentation just as dearly as he loves vegetation.

—RALPH WALDO EMERSON

APPLE CIDER VINEGAR

Makes 2 quarts (½ gallon)

Fermentation time: 6 to 8 weeks

Apple cider vinegar is a fermented vinegar made from crushed apples. Through a two-step fermentation process, the fruit's natural sugars are first converted into alcohol, then transformed by beneficial bacteria into acetic acid, which provides the vinegar's distinctive sharp flavor. Unfiltered vinegar contains the "mother," which is a collection of proteins, enzymes, and probiotics that form naturally during fermentation.

Apple cider vinegar contains probiotics, which support digestion, and acetic acid, which may help regulate blood sugar, as well as potassium and antioxidants. It's valued not only as a culinary ingredient but also as a natural health remedy when diluted with water or tea.

(continued)

Special equipment

2 (2-quart/½-gallon) glass jars

Cotton cloth and rubber band

Bottles with tight-fitting lids, for storing

Ingredients

Apple peels and cores from 6 to 8 apples or chopped whole apples, preferably a mixture of sweet and tart apples

½ cup sugar

2 quarts filtered water

1 tablespoon store-bought organic apple cider vinegar (optional)

1. Place the apple peels and cores in a jar, filling it about ¾ full.

2. In a large bowl, dissolve the sugar in the water. Add the apple cider vinegar, if using, to encourage fermenting. Pour the liquid over the apples to fully submerge, leaving 1 inch of space at the top.

3. Cover the jar with the cloth and secure with the rubber band. Store the jar in a dark place at room temperature (65°F to 75°F/18°C to 24°C) for 2 weeks, checking and stirring the mixture every day to prevent mold from forming on the surface.

4. After 2 weeks, strain out the solids. Transfer the liquid to a clean jar. Cover it again with the cloth and secure with the rubber band. Leave it to ferment in a dark place at room temperature (65°F to 75°F/18°C to 24°C) for another 4 to 6 weeks, stirring occasionally and tasting for doneness. Over time, it will develop a stronger vinegar scent and the "mother" may begin to form.

5. Once it tastes sharp and vinegary to your liking, transfer the vinegar to a bottle with a tight-fitting lid. Store in a cool, dark place. It will keep for up to 1 year and continue to mellow over time.

APPLE CIDER VINAIGRETTE

Makes about ¾ cup

This sharp and fruity vinaigrette is autumn forward. It's light enough to dress a leafy garden salad while robust enough to drizzle over hearty grain, legume, and crucifer salads.

Ingredients

¼ cup apple cider vinegar
1 tablespoon maple syrup
1 small garlic clove, grated
1 teaspoon Dijon mustard
¼ teaspoon kosher salt
⅛ teaspoon freshly ground black pepper
⅓ cup extra-virgin olive oil

1. Combine the vinegar, maple syrup, garlic, mustard, salt, and pepper in a small bowl and whisk to blend. Add the oil in a steady stream, whisking constantly to emulsify.

2. Store in the refrigerator for up to 2 days. Whisk to emulsify before serving.

RECIPES

INDIA AND THE MIDDLE EAST

Traditional fermented ingredients:
dairy, lentils, vegetables

INDIAN AND PAKISTANI MANGO LASSI

Makes 2 servings

Lassi is a yogurt-based drink from the Punjab region of India and Pakistan. It can be sweetened, blended with sugar, fruit, or rosewater, or savory, seasoned with salt, spices, and herbs. Lassi is traditionally served to aid digestion and balance the heat of spicy foods. It's both a nourishing and a hydrating drink, valued for its probiotic benefits and soothing, creamy texture.

Special equipment

Blender

Ingredients

1 cup chopped ripe mango or frozen chopped mango
1 cup plain whole milk yogurt
½ cup whole milk
1 tablespoon sugar or honey
⅛ teaspoon ground cardamom

Combine the ingredients in a blender. Blend until smooth and creamy. Taste and adjust the sweetness as needed. Refrigerate for up to 1 day. Serve with ice.

INDIAN DOSA

Makes 10 to 12 dosa

Fermentation time: 8 to 12 hours

Dosa (or *dosai*) are savory South Indian crepes made from a fermented gluten-free batter of rice and lentils. *Dosa* are light and crisp, with a tangy flavor that develops as the batter ferments and fills with air pockets. The rice and lentils provide a good source of protein and fiber, and the natural fermentation process promotes beneficial gut bacteria and boosts the availability of B vitamins. *Dosa* are traditionally served with chutney and sambar, a spiced lentil-and-vegetable stew.

Dal and fenugreek seeds are available online and in Asian specialty stores and well-stocked supermarkets.

Special equipment

Fine-mesh strainer
Wet grinder or powerful blender (such as Vitamix)
Kitchen towel

Ingredients

2 cups uncooked basmati rice
½ cup split urad dal (black gram lentils)
2 tablespoons chana dal (split chickpeas, optional)
1 teaspoon fenugreek seeds
1½ teaspoons kosher salt (see note)
Vegetable oil or ghee or, for pan-frying

1. Place the rice in a fine-mesh strainer and rinse under cool water. Transfer to a bowl and cover with at least 2 inches of filtered water. Place the urad dal and chana dal in the strainer and rinse under cool water. Transfer to a separate bowl. Add the fenugreek seeds to the dal and cover with at least 2 inches of filtered water. Let the rice and dal stand, uncovered, at room temperature for 8 to 12 hours.

(continued)

2. Drain the dal and fenugreek seeds, reserving some of the water. Grind until light and smooth, adding water 1 teaspoon at a time, to achieve a light and smooth consistency.

3. Drain the rice and grind until smooth and slightly grainy. Combine the dal and rice in a bowl and add enough water to achieve a pourable pancake-like batter.

4. Cover the bowl with a kitchen towel and place in a warm place (80°F to 90°F/26°C to 32°C), such as an oven with the pilot light on, with the door cracked for air circulation. Let the batter ferment for 8 to 12 hours, until puffed and nearly doubled in size, with small frothy bubbles all over the surface.

5. Add the salt and gently stir the batter. It should be thick but pourable in consistency. Add a little water to thin as needed.

6. Heat a nonstick or cast-iron skillet over medium-high heat until hot. Drizzle a few drops of oil in the pan, then carefully wipe the pan with a paper towel to coat the pan and absorb any excess oil.

7. Ladle about ½ cup of batter in the center of the skillet and quickly spread it outward in a spiral motion to form a round, thin pancake, about 9 inches in diameter.

8. Drizzle a few drops of oil around the edges. Cook for 3 to 4 minutes, until the bottom turns golden and crisp and the *dosa* looks cooked through. Fold and serve hot. Repeat with the remaining batter.

Note: Salt can inhibit fermentation, so it should be added only after the batter has fermented.

LEBANESE PICKLED TURNIPS

Makes 1 quart

Fermentation time: 5 to 7 days

Fermented pickled vegetables (*kabees*) are a staple in Lebanese cuisine and are often served with every meal. The pickled vegetables are traditionally fermented using the natural bacteria on the vegetables and a saltwater brine to transform them. During fermentation, the bacteria convert sugars into lactic acid, which acts as a preserver, providing probiotic benefits and creating a tangy flavor. Sliced beets are added to the brining solution to tint the vegetables a vibrant pink color. In addition to turnips, other vegetables can be pickled in this manner, including carrots, cauliflower, and Persian cucumbers.

Special equipment

1-quart glass jar with lid or airlock lid

Ingredients

1½ pounds turnips, peeled and cut into 1½-inch batons
1 small beet, peeled and sliced (for color)
4 garlic cloves, halved
2 cups filtered water
1 cup white vinegar
2 tablespoons coarse kosher salt

1. Layer the turnips, beet, and garlic into the jar. Pack tightly but don't crush.

2. Combine the water, vinegar, and salt in a medium bowl. Stir until the salt dissolves.

3. Pour the brine over the vegetables, making sure everything is submerged. Leave about 1 inch of space at the top. Loosely seal the jar or use an airlock lid following the manufacturer's instructions.

4. Let the turnips stand at room temperature (65°F to 75°F/18°C to 24°C) for 5 to 7 days, making sure they remain submerged. The liquid will turn pink, and the turnips will become tangy and crisp-tender.

(continued)

5. When pickled to your taste, store the jar in the refrigerator for up to 1 month; the flavors will continue to develop. Serve the pickles as part of an appetizer spread or a salad, as a side dish, or as a topping on sandwiches and wraps.

The earliest records of pickling date back to Mesopotamia around 2400 BCE, with cucumbers pickled in the Tigris Valley as early as 2030 BCE.

MOROCCAN PRESERVED LEMONS

Makes 1 quart

Fermentation time: 3 to 4 weeks

Preserved lemons are fresh lemons that have been brined in their juice and salt, undergoing a lacto-fermentation process that suppresses harmful bacteria and encourages beneficial bacteria to thrive, providing natural probiotics. This process softens the lemons and mellows their acidity, while their flavor becomes salty, sour, and concentrated. Preserved lemons are a staple condiment in North African and Middle Eastern cuisine, where they are added to stews, tagines, salads, and sauces.

Special equipment

1-quart glass jar with lid or airlock lid

Ingredients

6 to 8 large organic Meyer or Eureka lemons, washed and dried

½ cup kosher salt, divided

Fresh lemon juice, as needed

(continued)

1. Cut about 1/4 inch off the top and bottom of the lemons. Cut each lemon into quarters partway through so that they remain connected at the bottom.

2. Pack 2 teaspoons of the salt in each lemon. Pack the lemons in the jar, sprinkling the remaining salt between the layers and pressing to release some of the lemon juice. Top with additional lemon juice to completely cover the lemons.

3. Loosely seal the jar or use an airlock lid according to the manufacturer's instructions and let stand at room temperature (65°F to 75°F/18°C to 24°C) for 3 to 4 weeks, gently shaking the jar to distribute the juices every few days. The lemons are ready when they are soft and translucent. Seal the jar tightly and refrigerate for up to 6 months.

A classic lactic acid–fermented pickle creates its own acidity as it ferments over several days at room temperature.

ROASTED SALMON WITH PRESERVED LEMON GREMOLATA

Serves 2

In addition to salmon, the gremolata can be served with other thick fish, such as swordfish or halibut. It can also be served as an appetizer or as part of a meze, spooned over crostini or pita bread. It's best eaten within a day of preparation. Store in the refrigerator until use.

Preserved Lemon Gremolata

Makes 1 cup

½ cup finely chopped pitted green olives, such as Castelvetrano
¼ cup finely chopped Italian parsley leaves
¼ cup finely chopped preserved lemon rind plus 1 tablespoon brine liquid
2 tablespoons chopped toasted pine nuts
1 tablespoon drained capers
2 teaspoons extra-virgin olive oil
1 small garlic clove, grated

Roasted Salmon

2 (6-ounce) salmon filets, with or without skin, pinbones removed

Extra-virgin olive oil

Kosher salt and freshly ground black pepper

1. To make the gremolata, combine all the ingredients in a medium bowl. Mix and set aside.

2. Heat the oven to 400°F. Line a rimmed baking sheet with parchment paper.

3. To make the roasted salmon, arrange the salmon on the baking sheet, skin side down. Brush the salmon with the olive oil and season with the salt and pepper.

4. Bake the salmon for 15 to 20 minutes, depending on thickness, until opaque through the center.

5. Transfer to serving plates and spoon the gremolata over the fish.

RECIPES

AMERICAS

Traditional fermented ingredients:
corn, quinoa, *maca,* cacao, fruits, sugar

MEXICAN TEPACHE

Makes about 3 quarts

Fermentation time: 24 to 48 hours

Tepache is a fermented Mexican beverage originating in pre-Columbian Mexico. It's a lightly alcoholic, sweet-tart beverage that is served chilled. It's made from fermented pineapple peels and cores and piloncillo, which is an unrefined cane sugar with a deep molasses flavor.

The fermentation process relies on naturally occurring yeast and bacteria present on the pineapple peels. The sugar is the nutrient source for the microbes, which produce lactic acid and carbon dioxide, providing light effervescence to the drink. Tepache contains probiotics, which can benefit gut health, and vitamin C from the pineapple.

Special equipment

1-gallon jar with lid or airlock lid
Glass jars or bottles for storing

Ingredients

12 cups filtered water, divided
⅔ cup packed piloncillo or dark brown sugar
1 large ripe organic pineapple, thoroughly washed
3 cinnamon sticks
1 teaspoon cloves

1. Combine 2 cups of the water and the piloncillo in a saucepan over medium heat and stir to dissolve the sugar. Remove from the heat and cool to room temperature.

2. Cut off and discard the top and bottom of the pineapple. Trim the skin from the pineapple and remove the core. (Reserve the fruit of the pineapple for another use.)

(continued)

3. Cut the skins and core into large chunks. Place in the jar. Add the cinnamon and cloves. Pour the prepared sugar syrup into the jar, then cover with the remaining water, about 10 cups, to cover the skins and core, leaving at least 1 inch of space at the top. Loosely seal the jar or use an airlock lid according to the manufacturer's instructions and let stand at room temperature (65°F to 75°F/18°C to 24°C) for 24 hours.

4. After 24 hours, check the tepache. It should be slightly carbonated, tart, and mildly sweet. Drink as is or, for more strength, let it continue to ferment at room temperature (65°F to 75°F/18°C to 24°C) for an additional 12 to 24 hours. When ready to your taste, strain and discard all the solids. Transfer the liquid to clean glass jars or bottles with lids or caps. Store in the refrigerator for up to 1 week.

PERUVIAN CHICHA DE MACA

Makes about 5 cups

Fermentation time: 2 to 4 days

Chicha de Maca is a fermented Peruvian drink. It's a refreshing chilled beverage, incorporating *maca,* which is a root vegetable native to the high Andes of Peru. *Maca* is rich in carbohydrates and minerals, including iron, calcium, zinc, potassium, and copper as well as B vitamins and vitamins C and E. When the *maca* root undergoes fermentation, its nutritional profile is enhanced. *Maca* powder is available online, in well-stocked supermarkets, and in health food stores.

Special equipment

1½-quart glass jar with lid or airlock lid
Bottles for storing

(continued)

Ingredients

½ cup maca powder
5 cups filtered water
¼ cup packed piloncillo or dark brown sugar
1 (3 to 4-inch) cinnamon stick
3 cloves
Peels from apple, pineapple, or pear (to help natural fermentation, optional)
1 tablespoon active culture, such as unflavored kombucha (to kickstart fermentation, optional)

1. Combine the *maca*, water, piloncillo, cinnamon, cloves, and peels, if using, in a large pot. Slowly bring to a boil over medium-high heat, stirring to dissolve the *maca*. Gently simmer over medium heat for 30 minutes to develop the flavor. Remove from the heat and cool to room temperature.

2. Strain and discard the cinnamon, cloves, and any peels. Pour the liquid into the jar, leaving 1 inch of space at the top. Add the active culture, if using.

3. Loosely seal the jar or use an airlock lid according to the manufacturer's instructions. Let ferment at room temperature (65°F to 75°F/18°C to 24°C) for 2 to 4 days, to your desired taste. It should be lightly fizzy. Strain into bottles and refrigerate for up to 1 week.

SALVADORAN CURTIDO

Makes about 2 quarts

Fermentation time: 2 to 4 days

Curtido is a slightly fermented cabbage slaw. It's a traditional condiment in El Salvador and other Central American countries, often served with dishes such as pupusas (savory stuffed tortillas). *Curtido* is fermented using a process in which naturally present bacteria, primarily of the *Lactobacillus* genus, convert sugars in the vegetables into lactic acid. This process creates a sour flavor and helps to preserve the *curtido*. *Curtido* is a good source of probiotics, which can aid in digestion and contribute to a healthy microbiome.

Special equipment

2-quart glass jar with lid
Fermentation weight

Ingredients

4 cups filtered water, plus more as needed

1 medium head green cabbage (about 2 pounds), cored and finely shredded

2 medium carrots, peeled and shredded

1 small sweet onion, halved and thinly sliced

1 to 2 jalapeño peppers, seeded and finely diced

1 cup apple cider vinegar or white vinegar

1 tablespoon kosher salt

1 teaspoon dried oregano, preferably Mexican

1 teaspoon sugar

1. Heat the water in a large saucepan until very hot but not boiling. Place the cabbage in a strainer. Pour the water over the cabbage, then drain well.

2. Transfer the cabbage to a large bowl. Add the carrot, onion, and jalapeños and toss to combine.

3. Whisk the vinegar, salt, oregano, and sugar in a small bowl.

(continued)

4. Pack the vegetables into the jar. Pour the vinegar mixture over the vegetables and press down on the vegetables to submerge them in the liquid. (It should be juicy. If needed, add a little filtered water to completely cover the vegetables.) Leave 1 to 2 inches of space at the top.

5. Add the fermentation weight to weigh down the vegetables. Loosely seal with the lid or use an airlock lid following the manufacturer's instructions. Let stand at room temperature (65°F to 75°F/18°C to 24°C) for 2 to 4 days. After 2 days, check for taste. When ready, seal the lid tightly and refrigerate for up to 1 month.

MEXICAN HOT FERMENTED CACAO

Makes 1 to 2 servings

Most commercial chocolate is made with fermented cocoa beans that have undergone a fermentation process after being harvested from their pods. The beans are fermented and then roasted. The fermentation process involves yeast and bacteria that break down the pulp surrounding the cocoa beans. This process takes five to seven days to develop the chocolate flavor, aroma, and color and reduce some of the bitterness.

Raw cacao beans are fermented and dried—not roasted—which preserves their more natural characteristics. Their flavor is more intense, earthy, and bitter. Because they are not roasted, they retain more nutrients.

Ingredients

2 cups whole or 2% milk
2 tablespoons raw cacao powder
1 tablespoon maple syrup or brown sugar
¼ teaspoon pure vanilla extract
Pinch of sea salt
Pinch of ground cinnamon and/or cayenne (optional)

Combine the milk, cacao, maple syrup, vanilla, and salt in a medium saucepan over medium heat. Gently warm the milk, whisking frequently to blend the ingredients and prevent scalding. Do not let it boil. Taste and adjust the flavors and sweetness to your taste. Add the cinnamon and/or cayenne, if using. Serve warm.

RECIPES

AFRICA

Traditional fermented ingredients:
millet, teff, sorghum, cassava, honey

ETHIOPIAN AND ERITREAN INJERA

(FERMENTED FLATBREAD)

Makes 6 to 8 flatbreads

Fermentation time: 2 to 3 days

Injera is a fermented flatbread that serves as both a plate and a utensil for scooping food. It's deeply rooted in cultural tradition and meant to be shared and eaten communally. Injera is traditionally made with teff flour that is fermented over several days. The fermentation develops injera's characteristic sour flavor and airy texture. It also boosts its nutritional value by reducing the phytates (which can hinder the absorption of certain minerals in the digestive system) in teff and unlocking minerals such as iron and calcium, improving digestibility. Teff flour is available online and in well-stocked supermarkets and health food stores.

Injera is naturally gluten free and high in fiber. Serve injera with lentils, vegetables, or meat dishes, or serve as a base (plate) for shared meals to soak up sauces and flavor.

Special equipment

Large bowl with a lid
Kitchen towel

Ingredients

2 cups teff flour (preferably whole grain)
2½ cups filtered water, plus more as needed
1 tablespoon plain yogurt (to help kickstart fermentation, optional)
Pinch of salt
Vegetable oil or ghee, for pan-frying

1. Combine the teff and water in the large bowl. Stir until smooth. Stir in the yogurt, if using.

2. Loosely cover with a lid and let stand at room temperature (65°F to 75°F/18°C to 24°C) for 2 to 3 days, stirring once a day. When the batter is ready, it will be bubbly and tangy with a slightly sour aroma.

3. Skim any collected liquid from the top, then stir in the salt. The batter should be the consistency of a thin pancake batter; if too thick, add a little water.

(continued)

4. Heat a large nonstick or lightly oiled cast-iron skillet over medium heat. Pour a thin layer of batter in a circular motion, starting in the center and spiraling out. Tilt and swirl the pan to spread the batter evenly.

5. Cover and cook for 1 to 2 minutes without flipping. The injera is done when bubbles have formed on the surface and the edges lift. Transfer to a clean kitchen towel to cool. Repeat with the remaining batter.

6. Serve warm or at room temperature with stews, lentils, vegetables, or meat dishes.

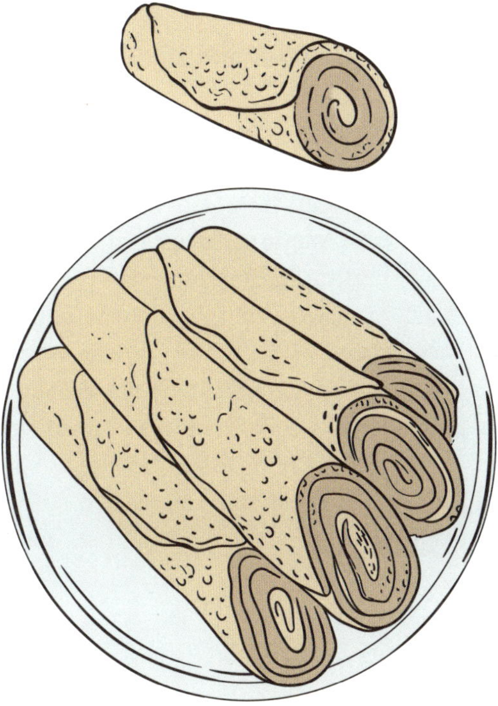

NIGERIAN OGI
(FERMENTED PORRIDGE)

Makes about 4 servings

Fermentation time: 3 days

Ogi is a traditional West African fermented cereal pudding made from maize, sorghum, or millet. The cereal grains are soaked for several days, allowing natural lactic acid bacteria to flourish, which softens the grains and boosts digestibility while providing a characteristic sour flavor and smooth texture. This fermentation process enriches the porridge with probiotics and makes nutrients more bioavailable.

Ogi is traditionally served warm and sweetened, with milk, for breakfast or paired with savory dishes such as *moin moin* (steamed boiled bean pudding) or fried plantains.

Special equipment

Food processor or blender

Cotton cloth

1 to 1½-liter glass jar with lid or airlock lid

Ingredients

2 cups hulled millet

Filtered water, for soaking, plus 3 cups, divided, and more as needed

Pinch of salt (optional)

Sugar or honey and milk, for serving

1. Rinse the millet under cold water. Drain and transfer to a large bowl and cover with 2 to 3 inches of water. Soak at room temperature for 24 hours to soften the grains.

2. Drain the millet. Transfer to a food processor and process to form a smooth paste, adding a little water if needed.

(continued)

3. Combine the millet paste with 1 cup of the water in the jar. Loosely cover with the cloth or use an airlock lid following the manufacturer's instructions and let stand at room temperature (65°F to 75°F/18°C to 24°C) for 2 days, stirring once or twice. The millet is ready when it begins to bubble and smell slightly sour.

4. Transfer the millet to a medium saucepan and whisk in the remaining 2 cups water. Simmer over medium heat until soft and creamy, about 15 minutes, stirring constantly. Add more water as needed to thin to your desired consistency. Season with a pinch of salt, if desired.

5. Serve warm with sugar or honey and milk.

Palm wine is an alcoholic drink made from the sap of various palm trees, which include date palms, coconut palms, and palmyra palms. It's a common beverage in parts of Africa, the Caribbean, South America, South Asia, Southeast Asia, and Micronesia. The sap, which naturally contains sugars, is collected from palm trees by tapping into the crown. The collected sap is left to ferment in sealed containers, where natural yeasts and bacteria convert the sugars into alcohol. The alcohol content of palm wine can range from about 2% to 15% ABV, depending on how long it ferments. Palm wine can also be distilled to create stronger spirits like *ogogoro* in Nigeria.

METRIC CONVERSIONS & EQUIVALENTS

METRIC CONVERSION FORMULAS

To Convert	Multiply
Ounces to grams	Ounces by 28.35
Pounds to kilograms	Pounds by .454
Teaspoons to milliliters	Teaspoons by 4.93
Tablespoons to milliliters	Tablespoons by 14.79
Fluid ounces to milliliters	Fluid ounces by 29.57
Cups to milliliters	Cups by 240
Cups to liters	Cups by .236
Pints to liters	Pints by .473
Quarts to liters	Quarts by .946
Gallons to liters	Gallons by 3.785
Inches to centimeters	Inches by 2.54

OVEN TEMPERATURES

To convert Fahrenheit to Celsius, subtract 32 from Fahrenheit, multiply the result by 5, then divide by 9.

Description	Fahrenheit	Celsius	British Gas Mark
Very cool	200°	95°	0
Very cool	225°	110°	¼
Very cool	250°	120°	½
Cool	275°	135°	1
Cool	300°	150°	2
Warm	325°	165°	3
Moderate	350°	175°	4
Moderately hot	375°	190°	5
Fairly hot	400°	200°	6
Hot	425°	220°	7
Very hot	450°	230°	8
Very hot	475°	245°	9

APPROXIMATE METRIC EQUIVALENTS

Volume

¼ teaspoon	1 milliliter
½ teaspoon	2.5 milliliters
¾ teaspoon	4 milliliters
1 teaspoon	5 milliliters
1¼ teaspoons	6 milliliters
1½ teaspoons	7.5 milliliters
1¾ teaspoons	8.5 milliliters
2 teaspoons	10 milliliters
1 tablespoon (½ fluid ounce)	15 milliliters
2 tablespoons (1 fluid ounce)	30 milliliters
¼ cup	60 milliliters
⅓ cup	80 milliliters
½ cup (4 fluid ounces)	120 milliliters
⅔ cup	160 milliliters
¾ cup	180 milliliters
1 cup (8 fluid ounces)	240 milliliters
1¼ cups	300 milliliters
1½ cups (12 fluid ounces)	360 milliliters
1⅔ cups	400 milliliters
2 cups (1 pint)	480 milliliters
3 cups	720 milliliters
4 cups (1 quart)	0.96 liter
1 quart plus ¼ cup	1 liter
4 quarts (1 gallon)	3.8 liters

Weight

¼ ounce	7 grams
½ ounce	14 grams
¾ ounce	21 grams
1 ounce	28 grams
1¼ ounces	35 grams
1½ ounces	42.5 grams
1⅔ ounces	47 grams
2 ounces	57 grams
3 ounces	85 grams
4 ounces (¼ pound)	113 grams
5 ounces	142 grams
6 ounces	170 grams
7 ounces	198 grams
8 ounces (½ pound)	227 grams
16 ounces (1 pound)	454 grams
35.25 ounces (2.2 pounds)	1 kilogram

Length

⅛ inch	3 millimeters
¼ inch	6.25 millimeters
½ inch	1.25 centimeters
1 inch	2.5 centimeters
2 inches	5 centimeters
2½ inches	6.25 centimeters
4 inches	10 centimeters
5 inches	12.75 centimeters
6 inches	15.25 centimeters
12 inches (1 foot)	30.5 centimeters

Information compiled from a variety of sources, including *Recipes into Type* by Joan Whitman and Dolores Simon (Newton, MA: Biscuit Books, 1993); *The New Food Lover's Companion* by Sharon Tyler Herbst (Hauppauge, NY: Barron's, 2013); and *Rosemary Brown's Big Kitchen Instruction Book* (Kansas City, MO: Andrews McMeel, 1998).

There in wine
is found the great
generalization:
All life is
fermentation.

—RICHARD FEYNMAN

ABOUT THE AUTHOR

Lynda Balslev is an award-winning cookbook author and food and drinks writer who is passionate about sharing her knowledge through the lens of travel and culture. Lynda is the author of six books, including *The Little Book of Fika, The Little Book of Dumplings,* and *Almonds: Recipes, History, Culture*. She currently writes a nationally syndicated food column and blog, *TasteFood*. Her work has appeared in various print and digital media, including NPR, *Culture, Eating Well, Relish,* and *Parade* magazine.

THE LITTLE BOOK OF FERMENTED FOODS

The authorised representative in the EEA is Simon and Schuster Netherlands BV, Herculesplein 96 3584 AA Utrecht, Netherlands. (info@simonandschuster.nl)

Andrews McMeel Publishing
a division of Andrews McMeel Universal
1130 Walnut Street, Kansas City, Missouri 64106

www.andrewsmcmeel.com

26 27 28 29 30 RLP 10 9 8 7 6 5 4 3 2 1

ISBN: 979-8-8816-0560-5

Library of Congress Control Number: 2025949722

Editor: Jean Z. Lucas
Illustrator: Irina Vaneeva
Art Director: Holly Swayne
Production Editor: Kayla Overbey
Production Manager: Chadd Keim

FSC
www.fsc.org
MIX
Paper | Supporting responsible forestry
FSC® C102842